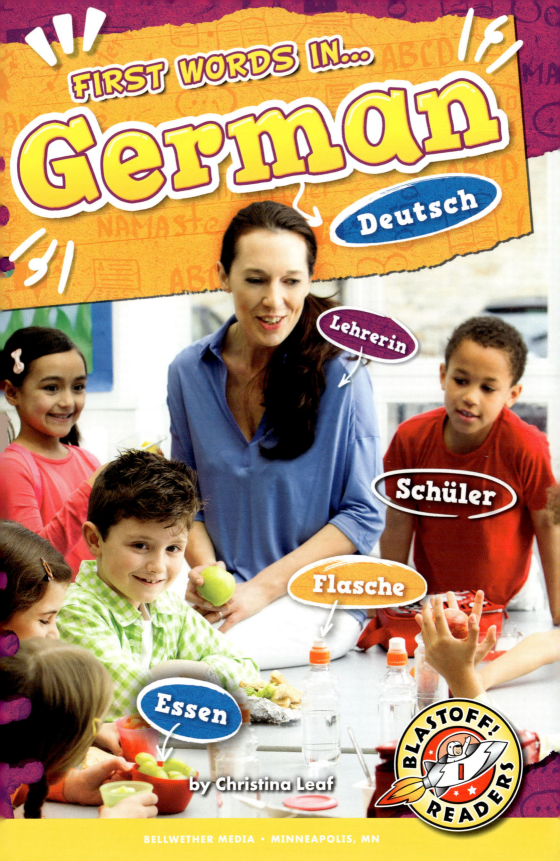

Blastoff! Readers are carefully developed by literacy experts to build reading stamina and move students toward fluency by combining standards-based content with developmentally appropriate text.

 Level 1 provides the most support through repetition of high-frequency words, light text, predictable sentence patterns, and strong visual support.

 Level 2 offers early readers a bit more challenge through varied sentences, increased text load, and text-supportive special features.

 Level 3 advances early-fluent readers toward fluency through increased text load, less reliance on photos, advancing concepts, longer sentences, and more complex special features.

★ **Blastoff! Universe**

This edition first published in 2026 by Bellwether Media, Inc.

No part of this publication may be reproduced in whole or in part without written permission of the publisher. For information regarding permission, write to Bellwether Media, Inc., Attention: Permissions Department, 3500 American Blvd W, Suite 150, Bloomington, MN 55431.

Library of Congress Cataloging-in-Publication Data

LC record for German available at: https://lccn.loc.gov/2025018589

Text copyright © 2026 by Bellwether Media, Inc. BLASTOFF! READERS and associated logos are trademarks and/or registered trademarks of Bellwether Media, Inc. Bellwether Media is a division of FlutterBee Education Group.

Editor: Suzane Nguyen   Designer: Andrea Schneider

Printed in the United States of America, North Mankato, MN.

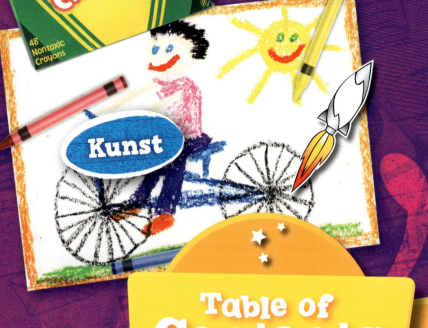

Table of Contents

Guten Tag!	4
At Home	8
At School	12
In the Evening	16
Tschüß!	20
Glossary	22
To Learn More	23
Index	24

Guten Tag!

Guten Tag! Ich heiße Greta. I speak *Deutsch*. Do you want to learn?

ß = ss
as in "pass"

Words to Know

- Guten Tag (GOOT-en tahg)......................hello/good day
- Ich heiße (ick HI-suh)...........my name is
- Deutsch (DOY-tch).........................German
- hallo (HAH-loh)..................................hello
- bitte (BIT-tuh)....please/you're welcome
- danke (DAHN-kuh)......................thank you

People in many countries speak German. They live in central and western Europe.

At Home

Hans lives with his *Eltern* and *Hund*. This is his *Haus*.

Katze

Haus
Schwester
Bruder
Eltern

Words to Know

- Mutter (MOO-tah) .... mother
- Vater (FA-tah) .... father
- Eltern (EL-turn) .... parents
- Bruder (BROO-der) .... brother
- Schwester (SHVES-tah) .... sister
- Haus (HOWS) .... house
- Hund (HOONT) .... dog
- Katze (KAT-suh) .... cat

Emma eats an *Ei* for *Frühstück*. Her mother pours her *Apfelsaft*.

Brot

Words to Know

- Morgen (MORE-gehn) .... morning
- Frühstück (FREW-shtuhck) .... breakfast
- Ei (ai) .... egg
- Brot (broht) .... bread
- Apfelsaft (AP-fel-zahft) .... apple juice

Ei

At School

Henry rides his *Fahrrad* to *Schule*. His *Stadt* has many paths!

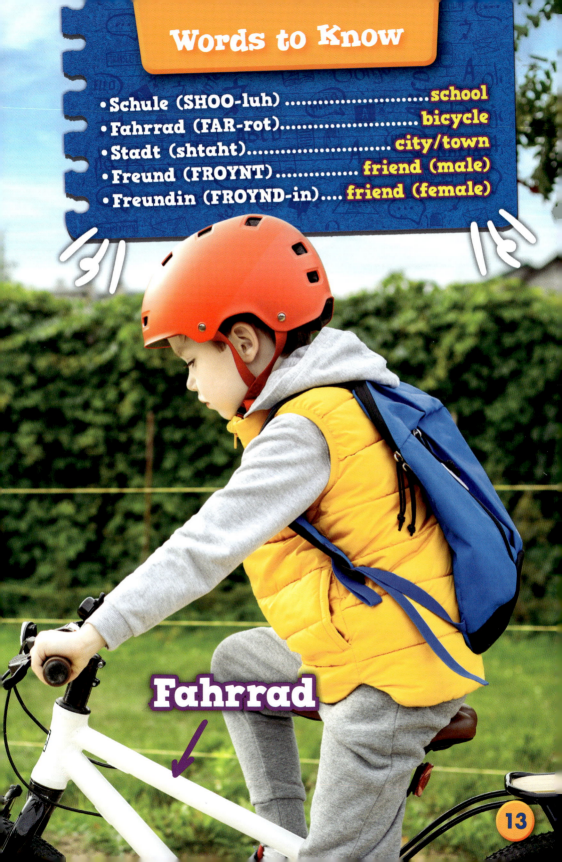

Words to Know

- Schule (SHOO-luh) .... school
- Fahrrad (FAR-rot) .... bicycle
- Stadt (shtaht) .... city/town
- Freund (FROYNT) .... friend (male)
- Freundin (FROYND-in) .... friend (female)

Fahrrad

Anna listens to her *Lehrerin* give **instructions**. She loves to make *Kunst*!

Lehrerin

Count in German

eins (EYENS).........1
zwei (TSVAI)............2
drei (DRY)............3
vier (FEER)...............4
fünf (FOONF)....5
sechs (ZECTS)............6
sieben (ZEE-bin)..7
acht (AKT)..................8
neun (NOYN)....9
zehn (TSAYN)...........10

Schülerin

Words to Know

- Lehrerin (LEY-ruh-rin)..teacher (female)
- Lehrer (LEY-rah)...............teacher (male)
- Schülerin (SHOO-ley-rin).............................student (female)
- Schüler (SHOO-leh)...........student (male)
- Klasse (KLAH-suh) ....class
- Kunst (koonst) ....art

15

In the Evening

Anders eats **schnitzel** for *Abendessen*. He has a glass of *Wasser*, too.

schnitzel

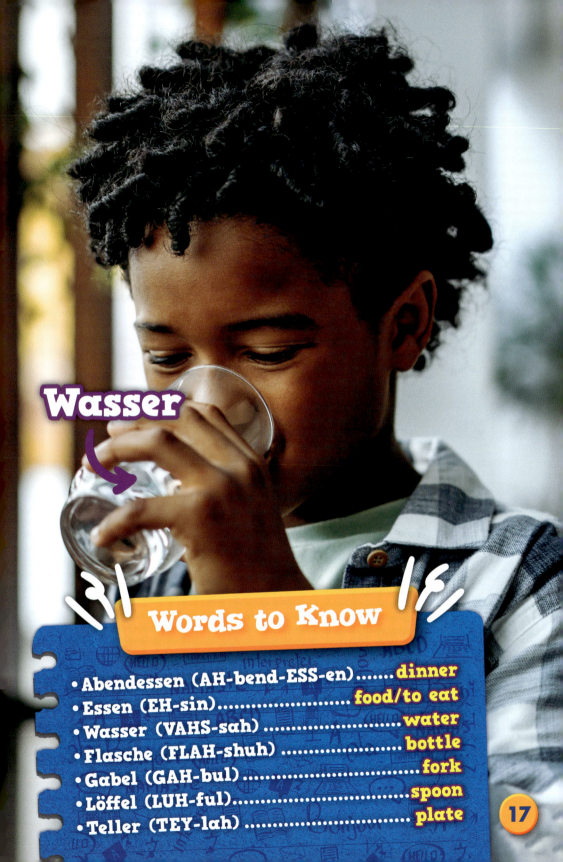

Wasser

Words to Know

- Abendessen (AH-bend-ESS-en) .... dinner
- Essen (EH-sin) .... food/to eat
- Wasser (VAHS-sah) .... water
- Flasche (FLAH-shuh) .... bottle
- Gabel (GAH-bul) .... fork
- Löffel (LUH-ful) .... spoon
- Teller (TEY-lah) .... plate

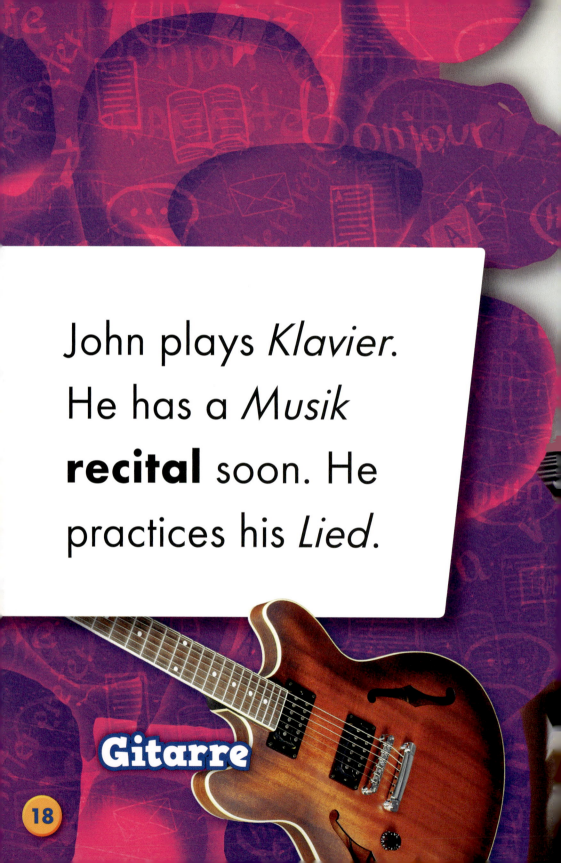

John plays *Klavier*. He has a *Musik* **recital** soon. He practices his *Lied*.

Gitarre

Klavier

Words to Know

- Klavier (CLA-veer) .... piano
- Lied (LEED) .... song
- Geige (GUY-guh) .... violin
- Musik (MOO-zeek) .... music
- Gitarre (gee-TAR-uh) .... guitar

19

Tschüß!

Katrina gets ready for *Bett*. It is time to *schlafen*. *Gute Nacht*!

Glossary

directions on what to do

a thin slice of meat that is often breaded and then fried

a music or dance event where people perform for others

To Learn More

AT THE LIBRARY

Barnes, Rachael. *Germany*. Minneapolis, Minn.: Bellwether Media, 2023.

DK. *German For Everyone Junior: 5 Words a Day*. New York, N.Y.: DK Publishing, 2021.

Gleisner, Jenna Lee. *My First Look at German*. Minneapolis, Minn.: Jump!, 2020.

ON THE WEB

FACTSURFER

Factsurfer.com gives you a safe, fun way to find more information.

1. Go to www.factsurfer.com.

2. Enter "German" into the search box and click 🔍.

3. Select your book cover to see a list of related content.

Index

count in German, 15

eats, 10, 16

Europe, 6

good night, 21

home, 8

learn, 4

map, 7

recital, 18

schnitzel, 16

school, 12, 14

sleep, 20

words to know, 5, 9, 11, 13, 15, 17, 19, 21

The images in this book are reproduced through the courtesy of: SolStock/ Getty Images, front cover; czarny_bez, p. 3; Irina WS, pp. 4-5; FamVeld, pp. 6-7; Nynke, p. 8 (Katze); anek.soowannaphoom, pp. 8-9; kwanchai.c, p. 10 (Brot); THESHOTS.CO, pp. 10-11; brusinski, pp. 12-13; wavebreak3, pp. 14-15; Esin Deniz, p. 16 (schnitzel); andreswd/ Getty Images, pp. 16-17; yrafoto, p. 18 (Gitarre); Yistocking, pp. 18-19; maemanee, pp. 20-21; tawanroong, p. 22 (instructions); shulers, p. 22 (recital); Brent Hofacker, p. 22 (schnitzel).